AF584818

A Scholastic Press book from Scholastic Australia

MY FEELINGS, MY RULES

NICKI ESLER GILL

KRUTI DESAI

For Mum and Dad, with love. – N.G.

To my son and mum, you have been my calm in the hard moments, and my joy in the bright ones. Thank you for being my constant love and support. – K.D.

Scholastic Press
An imprint of Scholastic Australia Pty Limited (ABN 11 000 614 577)
PO Box 579 Gosford NSW 2250
www.scholastic.com.au

Part of the Scholastic Group
Sydney · Auckland · New York · Toronto · London · Mexico City
New Delhi · Hong Kong · Buenos Aires · Puerto Rico

Published by Scholastic Australia in 2026.

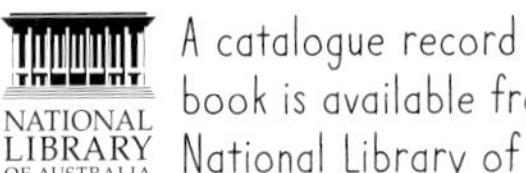

A catalogue record for this book is available from the National Library of Australia

ISBN: 978-1-76172-178-6

Typeset in Might Could Pencil and StrawberryMilkshake Medium.
The illustrations in this book were created digitally.
Book design by Laura Ye.

We acknowledge the Traditional Owners of the Country on which we live and work.
We pay respect to Elders past and present.

Printed in China by RR Donnelley.
Scholastic Australia's policy, in association with RR Donnelley, is to use papers that are renewable and made efficiently with wood from responsibly managed sources, so as to minimise its environmental footprint.

10 9 8 7 6 5 4 3 2 1 26 27 28 29 30 / 2

Have you ever had a **feeling**?
Or two or three or four?
Like joy, or love, or kindness,
and a **million** feelings more?

Have you ever felt a-tremble
at the most **exciting** part?

Or felt lovely, quiet **gladness**,
all for you, deep in your heart?

Have you ever had a **cuddle**
and felt you just might burst
with love for someone **special,**
who sees your best, not worst?

Have you ever clutched your teddy
when you're **worried** in the night?

Have you ever lost a race,

or have you ever had a **fight**?

Then, before you even knew it,
were your feelings on the mend?
Your tears all dry, and full of **fun,**
and playing with a friend?

That's how our feelings are, you see.
They **come** and then they **go.**
Try thinking of the apple tree—
its seasons **ebb and flow.**

At times the tree is **blossoming**
with sweetly smelling flowers.
And sometimes boughs are **bare,**
bobbing in the wind for hours.

Sometimes the tree is laden
full of juicy crunchy **treats**
to pick and munch and crunch upon—
a feeling nothing **beats!**

And all these ways are **healthy**
for an apple tree to be.
Just like the way our feelings **change**
is normal too, you see?

And sometimes storms will lash and toss.
And mighty gale wind **strikes!**

There's crashing,
booming **thunder**
paired with mighty flashing lights.

Your angry times may feel like this.
You'd like to storm and **shout!**
And tears may pour like pelting rain.
It's ok! **Ride it out.**

There are ways to **help** ourselves,
and you can learn them too,
so we don't **harm** each other
and so your storms won't hurt you.

Try noticing your feelings,
and then just let them **pass.**

Talk with someone who you love.

Walk barefoot on the grass.

Or move and groove and boogie
just to let the **crankies** out.

Try **nature** walks

or **pillow** slams
so you don't scream and shout!

Or notice something beautiful
you **see**, or **smell**, or **hear**.

Or simply have a cuddle
with a **grown-up** you hold dear.

And like the tree after the wind,
you'll still stand tall and **strong.**

Your storm will pass. The sun will shine.
More **fun** will come along!

We all feel joy and sorrow.
We all have **hopes and fears.**
We laugh and love and dream and wait,
and sometimes we cry **tears.**

It's just part of being **human**
in this wide and wondrous world.
And you are loved, with each and every
feeling **mixed** and swirled.

You're precious when you're happy,
and you're precious when you're **blue.**
With all your different feelings,
it's just part of being **you!**